Meaning
from
Madness

Richard Skerritt

Meaning
from
Madness

Understanding the Hidden Patterns
that Motivate Abusers:
Narcissists, Borderlines, and Sociopaths

Richard Skerritt

Dalkeith Press
Kennett Square, Pennsylvania, USA

Published in 2006 by

Dalkeith Press
873 East Baltimore Pike #742
Kennett Square, PA 19348 USA

Library of Congress Control Number: 2006904457

Softcover Edition:
ISBN10: 1-933369-14-0
ISBN13: 978-1-933369-14-3

Cover Image used under license from Corbis.

Sixth Printing, March 2016

Contents

Introduction

When I talk with people who have been in abusive relationships, people struggling to deal with the experience and move forward, I always have to help them make some sense of the behavior of the abusive person in their lives. Because of their disorders, abusers literally see the world differently than healthy people do. What abusers *do* see, they respond to very differently from healthy people.

This leads abusers to say and do things that make no sense from the perspective of a healthy person. But because it's very important for abusers to maintain the reality which they perceive, they use powerful persuasive methods in an effort to get us to accept their reality. Although we nearly always know that something is not right, we can become very seriously confused about what *is* real.

Explaining all this to someone who is living with it is a real challenge, and mostly I find the explanation focuses in three fundamental areas:

1) the psychological dynamics of personality disorders;

2) the nature and purpose of psychological defense mechanisms; and

3) the role and effect of substance abuse, especially alcoholism, in disordered

behavior.

This mini book is not an academic treatise. It is not based on scientific research. It is a simple, practical explanation of the dynamics of personality disordered abusers from the perspective of those who live with them. My purpose here is to provide in written form the same basic explanation I give to people when I write to or speak with them in a mentoring role. I hope to convey a framework for both cause-and-effect and motivation within the minds of disordered abusers. This I hope will give spouses, family, and intimate friends a sensible way of understanding and evaluating the behavior to which they are subjected. I also offer a summary of the possibilities for improvement with treatment and the probability of successful treatment.

There are detailed and accurate descriptions of mental illnesses and their symptoms available in other works, most notably the American Psychiatric Association's *Diagnostic and Statistic Manual of Mental Disorders, Text Revision, DSM-IV-TR*, published in 2000. My purpose here is not to be authoritative or comprehensive. While the general concepts I present should be in harmony with the more technical and complete descriptions, they are not intended to be substitutes for those technical descriptions. You can think of my essential dynamics as a way of explaining the more technical definitions.

2

Toward the end of the book, I include the definitions for the disorders discussed here, taken from the DSM-IV-TR. This is the authoritative definition of these disorders. I think it's important for family or people with other intimate relationships with a disordered person to review and assess these official diagnostic definitions.

This mini book is a complement to my book *Tears and Healing*, and can be used in parallel with it. *Tears and Healing* can guide you through the difficult emotional evaluations you need to make to understand your personal needs and desires in life. This book should give you the factual perspective on the disorder you're dealing with so that you have some reasonable sense of what the future may hold. Taken together, the emotional insight and the factual understanding will empower you to feel confident in choosing the future course for your life. If this work is successful, readers living with a disordered abuser will find clarity and confidence in assessing their situation and making decisions to move forward.

Notes

Meaning from Madness

The Paradox of Abusive Behavior

"Why would he do this to me?" "What could I have possibly done to deserve that from her?" Questions like these have been asked thousands of times, and will be asked thousands of times again in the future, by the countless anguished people struggling to understand the behavior of a spouse, partner, parent, child, or friend.

Sadly, their questions will remain unanswered until they learn a completely new perspective on what they are experiencing. These questions don't have answers because they are based on a faulty premise: they assume that the way a disordered abuser treats you has something to do with you. As we will see later, abusive behavior is all about what is happening inside the mind of the abuser, is based on a reality that the abuser distorts and controls, and often has little or nothing to do with the person who is subjected to it.

Imagine a mischievous programmer, with access to the program statements that control the behavior of a common word processor. Normally, pressing a "K" on the keyboard inserts a "K" into the document, but this programmer alters the invisible inner workings of the program. She alters the program to randomly associate keys with letters. Pressing

5

"K" now inserts a "W"; the next time perhaps an "I", and so on for each of the other keys. And yet, when starting the program, it looks just like the same word processor that we've come to know so well.

Now imagine that a perfectly intelligent and experienced user of this word processor - maybe someone like you - sits down and starts this familiar looking program. This user sees what appears to be a completely common and well-understood situation. Yet when the user begins to type, surprising things appear on the screen. Printing the resulting text confirms that the resulting document is far from what is expected.

"What is going on?! Why is this program doing this? When I type "A", an "S" or an "N" or an "H" appears. If I delete it and type again, then something else shows up! Why is this happening? What did I do wrong?"

Just like the questions asked in the opening paragraph, there are no answers to these questions – at least not in the frame of reference that they are asked. In both cases, the questioner is using the wrong map to navigate through the situation. The first question assumes that the other person is a normal, reasonably healthy person, and our poor computer victim is responding as if the program were a regular, properly functioning version of the word processor.

But in both cases, the invisible programming is far from normal. Impossible to see from outside, both the program and the person respond to events in the world according to rules or dynamic patterns which are actually fairly well defined, yet make absolutely no sense in the context of what is normal. From outside, at first blush, both seem normal, but when you really try to interact with them, both of them are, well... crazy.

Unknown to most of us, a substantial fraction of the people around us, the people who make up our world, are disordered. They suffer from what the professionals call personality disorders. At least as many have similar but less severe problems called disordered personality styles. Dealing with these people will always be painful and baffling until we learn to understand the rules governing their behavior.

Notes

The Wiring is Different

The invisible programming inside the minds of disordered people leads to the thoughts, feelings, and behaviors that we identify as characteristic of personality disorders. This wiring controls how events are perceived, remembered, and what kind of response they cause.

After all is said and done, when we talk about abusers, the most important realization is that *their minds simply do not work the same way ours do.* For most of us, achieving this understanding is difficult. To get there, we must accept that the world around us is not the same world we grew up to believe in.

Most of us were taught how to behave and how to treat others, something that can be simply put as "do to others as you would have them do to you." The problem is that, as rational beings, we expect that others should honor that same rule in the way they treat us.

STOP!

While true for many people, there are still a significant number who can't and won't treat us as we would treat them. They can't because they perceive an entirely different reality than we do. Standing in the same place, seeing and hearing the same events, the disordered have a totally different experience than we do. Their defense mechanisms block and distort the sensory input they receive, while their emotional wiring leads to extreme and frightening emotional states that motivate them to respond with desperate and hurtful behaviors.

They are living in a world that has drastic differences from our world, and they are wired to respond to what they perceive in ways that we can never explain or understand based on how we react to our world

Getting to the bottom of this will mean changing the way you look at people, and learning two new facets of mental illness. The first facet is the defense mechanisms which alter perception and memory. The second is made up of the psychological dynamics of personality disorders, which motivate people to extreme and puzzling behaviors. In dealing with abusers, we almost always see three personality disorders from what is called Cluster B in the official diagnostic definitions: borderline, narcissistic, and antisocial (sociopathic) personality disorders.

It makes the most sense to start with an understanding of the psychological dynamics, since these dynamics pervade and dictate most everything in the lives of the disordered. With that understanding, the defense mechanisms can be explained to show how these defenses protect the disordered from the things they fear.

Meaning from Madness

Notes

The Abusive Personality Disorders - A Visit To Another Planet

It all seems so right at first, and so familiar, when we first begin a relationship with a disordered person. Yet the inner workings of those with the abusive personality disorders are far from it. As our relationships progress, we're increasingly subjected to puzzling and hurtful behaviors. To cope, we must come to an understanding that they are not like us, and they operate according to perceptions and motivations that have little in common with those of healthier people around them.

In my work with people struggling with the effects that disordered, abusive SOs (significant others) cause, I consistently see three disorders on Cluster B of axis II of the APA (American Psychiatric Association) diagnostic classification system. These disorders are enduring patterns of seeing, feeling, interacting, and impulsively responding that cause significant difficulty living life. The APA calls such disorders personality disorders, and the three that consistently show up in abusers are borderline, narcissistic, and antisocial. Because these so consistently appear as the underlying cause of abusive behavior, I call them *the abusive disorders*.

It turns out that the abusive disorders fall at either end of a spectrum of sensitivity. On the extreme of being *hypersensitive* to interactions, those with both borderline and narcissistic personality disorders are subject to being triggered – responding with tremendous energy to a very small event or observation. On the opposite extreme of being *insensitive* to interactions, sociopaths (those with antisocial personality disorder) have little or no empathy, remorse or conscience. They care so little about what others think or feel that they are nearly completely free of any fear of the outcome or results of their actions. As a result, they may choose to do things that normal people find stunning in their callousness and insensitivity.

I'll present the official diagnostic definition of these illnesses later, as a sort of safety net. To start, I want to give you an *idea* what these disorders are about. I'm going to reduce each disorder to one fundamental psychological dynamic. A dynamic is like a wound spring; a source of tension that is constantly under stress, and sits ready to unleash its pent-up energy on the next unlucky person to touch that sensitivity. While the official definitions require four or more enduring behaviors, my experience suggests that using a single dynamic – an underlying motivation rather than a behavior – is an easier way to understand and recognize these three disorders.

Disorders of Fear: Borderline and Narcissism

I listen to the stories of many adults who are (or have been) in intimate relationships within abusive, disordered partners. They never describe behavior that I consider either pure narcissistic or pure borderline. As I've worked to understand these two disorders from the common perspective of the people living with them, I have come to believe that narcissistic personality disorder (NPD) and borderline personality disorder (BPD) are actually the same basic disorder. The differences between the two, as I see them, are different coping strategies and different levels of success in coping.

Both those with NPD (who I'll call NPs or narcissists for short) and those with BPD (who I'll refer to as BPs for short) are driven by a constant and deeply motivated drive to find safety in their lives by avoiding things that trigger their terrifying fears. Both narcissists and BPs perceive a threat in the judgments of the people around them, one that is so great that it is terrifying to them,

Moreover, events around these people, even the most insignificant, can take on great meaning. Statements or events that have absolutely no significance to us may signal an imminent and terrifying change to a BP or narcissist. This super-sensitivity to events which are interpreted as threatening is often baffling. In fact, we may not even realize something has happened to trigger these reactions, yet the reactions themselves are powerful and often very hurtful.

Both borderline personality disorder (BPD) and narcissistic personality disorder (NPD) have a fundamental dynamic of fear. Those with both disorders rely on a particular type of interaction to maintain their feeling of safety, and they are very hypersensitive to anything that threatens that interaction. For BPs, the key relationship is a committed partner that provides safety. Frightening and powerful fears are unleashed by anything that suggests that their committed partner will abandon them. A narcissist, in contrast, finds safety within a circle of people where the narcissist feels perceived as without fault. The same kind of frightening and powerful fears are unleashed by anything that might suggest or reveal the slightest flaw to those people.

I believe both these disorders are based in a fundamental recognition of the world as threatening, and a hypervigilance to protect against those threats. Narcissists muster a certain kind of defense to protect themselves, while BPs are more defenseless. I believe that, within the group of people suffering from these two disorders, everyone who is functioning at some reasonable level in the world is using narcissistic defenses and will appear mainly narcissistic. If the narcissistic defense breaks down, and it may since it's based on an impossible premise of being flawless, a borderline dynamic emerges. A "pure" borderline with no narcissistic defenses is likely to be dysfunctional in life or even hospitalized.

Notes

The Surprising Outward View of Narcissism

Of all the many, many stories I've read in the online support groups I've been part of since 2000, by far the most common hurtful behaviors are narcissistic. Even among those who believe their partner has BPD or another disorder, the common thread through most of the hurtful interactions is narcissistic.

Narcissism, because there really *is* a myth about Narcissus, is surrounded even today by a mythological cloak. In fact, this cloak almost completely obscures what I see as the fundamental dynamic of this personality disorder. The myth is interesting, but for our purposes here it serves only to outline something that NPD is not.

In myth, and in much popular conception, narcissists have grandiose views of themselves; they adore and love themselves; and in some current psychology circles, they are people trapped in a childlike stage of development. Though they may fit from the perspective of a casual observer, living with a narcissist gives lie to these beliefs.

Living with a narcissist shows the reality of NPD is this: narcissists believe themselves to be critically and fatally flawed, and they dread and fear the discovery of this reality by others. To protect themselves, they strain every muscle and expend every shred of energy to maintain their appearance as flawless. They feel, at a very deep level, that exhibiting the slightest flaw may be enough to reveal the true nature they believe of themselves: despicable and detestable people.

Because narcissists work so hard to be perfect, they are often powerful and successful people. They may work extremely hard at a job, a family position, or volunteer role. Nothing is too much to ask, and everything must be done to perfection. And other aspects of their lives, including self-care, may be totally neglected. I'll say more about this later in the "ins and outs".

Why perfection? We can't really know what is going on in the mind of a narcissist, but we can make a reasonable guess, and one that fits with the childhood experiences of many. If children are grossly mistreated for small errors in behavior, and if they are ignored or sometimes rewarded when they behave perfectly (according to *someone else's* perception - their parents'), they may develop a basic *dynamic* of feeling safe when others perceive them as perfect, and feeling very, *very* threatened when they think others will perceive them as deficient.

Narcissists have a common reaction to a threat to their image. Invariably, they react by discrediting, demeaning, derogating, and possibly destroying the person who challenged their image. In business settings, they may maintain an outward appearance of propriety, at the same time doing all they can to destroy the credibility of the person threatening their image.

For those unlucky enough to be behind closed doors with a threatened narcissist, the fear can erupt into violent rage. Whether this happens depends on whether you are "in" or "out" of where the narcissist draws the boundary between self and others. As long as you remain part of the others - the people with whom the narcissist seeks to maintain an image of perfection - the narcissist's reaction is likely to be measured. Once you move within the narcissist's definition of self, the reaction to a threat to the image can become brutal.

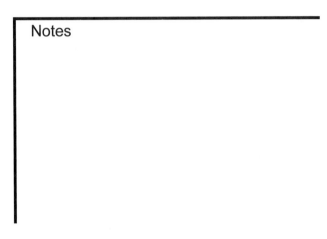

Notes

More Myth: Healthy Narcissism

Some psychodynamic approaches to narcissism
are based on the concept of narcissism as a love
of self. These approaches reason that since some
love of self is good, there is a "healthy
narcissism", and that the disease of narcissism
results from an excess of self love. I find this
approach both incorrect and distressing.

Narcissists don't love themselves too much.
They despise themselves, and most all of their
life energy is devoted to maintaining a false
image that covers this. This makes the idea of
"healthy narcissism" absurd. Narcissism is a
very serious illness; one that impairs almost all
aspects of emotional functioning. To be healthy
means to be free of this significant disorder.
There is no "healthy narcissism".

The Ins and Outs of Narcissism

The classic mythological definition of narcissism as self love leaves unexplained a significant feature of the disease. This feature is a nearly total dichotomy of treatment of others by narcissists.

As described earlier, narcissists seek to maintain an image of perfection among the people who surround them. To neighbors, coworkers, and acquaintances, narcissists often are considered wonderful and successful people. They are devoted to what they do, and excel in almost all aspects. They may show occasional failings, but these are more than made up for by their long history of fine achievements. Their reputations are built, in part, on the way they treat others. They may be very generous, patient, or cooperative. They have to be, because they need to be perceived by those around them as perfect. Any suggestion of imperfection is intensely frightening to them.

But when a person becomes closely associated with a narcissist, especially by marriage or being the child of a narcissist, a transition is crossed. Before the marriage, that person was a part of the "other" world of the narcissist, the world with which the narcissist tries to maintain an image of perfection. As a spouse or child, the person becomes *a part* of the narcissist's definition of self. When this happens, the dynamic changes completely. Before, the

narcissist made strenuous efforts to behave
perfectly toward the person, and asked only that
the other support this image. Now the narcissist
views the person as a *part* of his/her projected
self-image. It is no longer important how the
person views the narcissist; it is now imperative
that the person *also* present an impression of
perfection to those "outside".

Before, the only burden on the person was to be
agreeable to the narcissist's desired image.
Now, the burden is to become a part of it, and
do everything to satisfy the narcissist's
overwhelming need to show perfection. Without
knowing it, the now "included" other suddenly
is held to the same impossible standard that the
narcissist holds for him/her self. In effect, the
included other now bears the burden of
behaving like a narcissist, but lacks the
narcissist's compelling motivation to maintain
that behavior.

The need for approval from the person
evaporates; everything becomes secondary to
maintaining the image. And narcissists have a
high threshold for acceptable: perfection. Any
behavior or public visibility that suggests
anything less is intolerable. Imperfection in the
other person now also becomes an imminent
threat to the narcissist, and all measures to
achieve control become necessary. All flaws
must be eliminated, immediately. Intimidation,
criticism, manipulation, and rage can all be
employed to ensure the "self-included" other

person maintains the proper standard of behavior.

Moreover, the standard is itself an impossible one. There may not be anything that can be done that meets the narcissist's definition of perfect, and yet the narcissist may continue to abuse and drive the included other to be better. For the other person, the relationship may simply become one of constant abuse by the narcissist, seeking to erase a pain that lies in a fear of imperfection in a world where imperfection is everywhere and perfection is impossible.

A tremendous dichotomy of behavior may occur when the narcissist and included other move from a private setting to a public setting. At home, where no one "outside" can see, any level of emotional violence can be used by the narcissist to control the other. But in public, the narcissist's behavior is constrained to within socially acceptable limits. The "included" other will likely be treated with consideration and courtesy, since in public the narcissist's behavior must rise to the standard of perfection. Public mistakes by the other – that is, anything that the narcissist perceives as indicating a flaw – will be publicly corrected in an attempt to "fix" the perception caused by that mistake. But the brutal raging and controlling behavior is reserved for private settings.

Notes

Now You See It - Now You Don't

Because everyone is initially "outside" to a narcissist, the disease has a dumbfounding change for those unlucky enough to move from "outside" to "inside" the narcissist's self-definition. The outward perception that is sought by the narcissist is one of perfection, and this isn't limited to work performance.

Narcissists also strain every nerve to appear perfect when they engage in an intimate relationship. And since the need to be *perceived* as perfect is so strong, it overwhelms any inherent personality the narcissist may have. In other words, the behavior of a narcissist toward those "outside" is completely contrived. It is a conglomerate of behavior designed to impress.

Probably because they perceive such a great threat from the world around them, narcissists often become very adept at sensing the desires of those around them. After all, each person has their own likes and dislikes, and if a narcissist is to appear perfect to all, then having some idea of what people want is critically important. The narcissist can then adapt his/her behavior to match that desire, producing the perception of… perfection! This reading of others needs and adapting to match those needs is called *mirroring* (described later under defense mechanisms.)

Early in intimate relationships, narcissists often mirror the desires of their new partners. All too often, a new partner is swept right off his/her emotional feet, often declaring that the narcissist is everything they ever dreamed of. With their skill at reading others needs and reactions, and their intense desire to be perfect, it's no surprise that narcissists charm and disarm their new partners.

Of course, all this happens during a stage when the new partner is "outside" the narcissist's self-definition boundary. The charm and perfection of the early relationship disappears abruptly and the "now you don't" phase begins when the relationship is cemented (usually by marriage). The intimate partner now crosses to within the narcissist's self-definition boundary. The narcissist's need to mirror the partner stops and is replaced with a need to control the partner, as described above. Mirroring and perfection give way to abuse and control. The perfect partner suddenly becomes perfectly horrible.

Unfortunately for the partner, two things have

usually happened by this time. First, the partner has fallen hopelessly in love with the perfect "now you see it" version of the narcissist. Second, the partner has made serious joint commitments with the narcissist that can't easily be withdrawn. Faced with powerful feelings of love for the narcissist, and major shared commitments, the abrupt change in behavior is often tolerated. The partner now finds him/her self trapped in a situation that is unbearable, yet at the same time, leaving the situation is emotionally and/or practically impossible.

Not realizing that the future holds a life of terror, the partner will usually gut it out, trying to make things work. This sets the stage for the narcissist to work an extended campaign of reality distortion and brainwashing on the partner. By the time it becomes obvious that things will never get better and the situation exceeds normal human endurance, the partner is quite probably seriously confused about what is happening or what is right and wrong. At this point, exiting the abuse means exiting the relationship, and that requires clarity of thought, which the narcissist has worked to destroy. The fairy tale of the early relationship has become a grim story.

Notes

An Extreme of Dysfunction: Narcissism is a crippling and consuming disorder. The narcissist's terror of being found out is so overwhelming that virtually all normal emotional functioning is suppressed. Narcissists are characterized as lacking empathy. Actually, it is impossible to really know what normal-intensity emotions a narcissist has, because these are simply overwhelmed by the overriding fear of being found imperfect. It may be that a narcissist finds it necessary to project an image of being empathetic because this is what the narcissist believes those around him/her require to be perfect. Thus in this case empathy might be displayed in abundance where there is no empathy at heart. In the same way, in a setting like the military, a narcissist may find it necessary to behave without empathy, and would certainly do so, even if at heart empathy did exist. We simply cannot tell.

The bottom line with narcissism is that their lives are a lie. What they are; what they might care about; what feelings they have underneath their overriding fear; all these are a mystery. All that is given by the narcissist to those around is either a lie for those "outside", or intimidation, control, and abuse to those "within". What true character underlies the disease remains forever a mystery.

From Generation to Generation

NPD is transmitted strongly and in a stable way from parent to child.

As described above, spouse and children are drawn into the "inside" of the narcissist's self-definition. Thus, rather than the narcissist trying to convince spouse and children that the narcissist is flawless, spouse and children are expected by the narcissist to *also* project an image of flawlessness to the rest of the world.

Since the children (initially) are not narcissists and have no interest in appearing flawless, the narcissist parent must achieve control over them to make them do this.

Control is achieved by *punishing* any display of flaws. This is automatic for the NP since a child displaying a flaw causes the same fear reaction within the NP as if the NP had displayed the flaw. And "any" means any flaw perceived by the NP parent, and can include the most miniscule flaws of which the child may be totally unaware. Punishing generally means emotional brutality, i.e. abuse. Thus, this results in the child being brutalized for small errors, even when the child has no idea that he/she has done anything wrong.

The children are brutally punished for the slightest mistake, even when they don't know they made it. But like the narcissistic parent, they are safe when they are flawless. In time they learn to react to their world as one that will brutalize them for the slightest flaw, and one in which they are safe when they are without flaw. For some children with a predisposition or other environmental factors, this becomes ingrained at a level below conscious processing (as many trauma reactions are), and such a child matures to become a narcissist.

Then the child has children. And so it repeats, generation after generation, in a sad, pathetic destruction of human potential and happiness.

Notes

Nothing Borderline about BPD

Like narcissists, those with borderline personality disorder (BPD) operate under a fundamental dynamic of fear. While narcissists find safety in others' perception of them as flawless, those with BPD (who I'll also refer to as BPs for short) find safety in a relationship with a committed partner. Frightening and powerful fears are unleashed by the thought that their committed partner will abandon them.

And like narcissists, BPs are grossly hypersensitive. At heart they consider themselves despicable, and become hypervigilant in defense against perceived threats of abandonment resulting from the most minute form of criticism. In this way, the BP and narcissist dynamics are very similar. Both secretly consider themselves loathsome, and both fear the reaction of others when they discover this. Both are extremely hypersensitive, sensing imminent threat in events of the smallest significance. While narcissists seem to have a general fear of being found out, BPs have the specific fear that their committed partner will abandon them if they find out.

As we saw, the reaction of a narcissist to a threat is to either eliminate the threat, usually by controlling the threatening person, or to disarm the threat by discrediting the source of the threat. Because BPs are responding to a more specific fear, their reactions are different. Typically, when a BP fears abandonment, they will try to change the outcome of the threat rather than neutralize the threat. To do this, they will seek to either push or draw the other person back into a situation that feels more safe, or they will "head off at the pass" the threat of abandonment by abandoning the other person first.

In an effort to draw the abandoning SO back toward the BP, the BP may do what is informally called "hoovering". Hoovering is a no-holds-barred display of kindness, affection, and agreeableness intended to suck the SO back in, just like the vacuum cleaner of the same name. There is a lot of similarity here to the narcissists mirroring in the early stages of an intimate relationship. The narcissist however, will try to maintain that perfect image all the time, while the hoovering BP does it only long enough for the specific purpose of preventing the anticipated abandonment by their partner.

The BP may also invoke the approach behind the old maxim, "You can't fire me, I quit!" Depending on the BP's emotional state and how seriously the situation actually threatens to end the relationship, the BP may react to imminent abandonment by verbally brutalizing the abandoning partner. Here again there is a similarity to narcissism in that the BP is acting to destroy the credibility of the partner that the BP feels is abandoning them.

A third possibility falls along the lines of the defense mechanisms that are discussed later. In this reaction, the BP will "split the partner out of existence". This is really a combination of extreme devaluation which occurs with the defense mechanisms called splitting with diminished recall of events characteristic of the defense mechanism called dissociation. The BP will act as if the partner never existed and doesn't exist even when in the presence of the BP. Since there is no one there, then there is no way the BP could be abandoned now, or even could have been abandoned in the past. When the relationship has been an intimate one, this outcome can be extremely painful for the BP's partner.

In yet another possible reaction, one devoid of any effective defense mechanisms, the BP may respond to the perceived abandonment by simply collapsing in despair.

Notes

Overlap of BPD and Narcissism

There is significant overlap between BPD and narcissism. Both the BP and the narcissist are very sensitive to any flaws that others perceive in them. The narcissist develops an outer perimeter -- a protective shield of perceived perfection. The narcissist's energy is focused on maintaining that shield and the narcissist's fears focus on a breach of that shield. The narcissist, having a stronger outer perimeter, stands his ground and fights back against the revelation of a flaw.

A BP, on the other hand, lacks such an outer shield, and so the BP's fears are actually closer to their core or fundamental dread: that their protective partner will abandon them. BPs concede defeat as soon as a flaw is revealed and immediately react to the consequence they expect: to be abandoned by the person they most depend on. Instead of containing the revelation of the flaw, as the narcissist does, the BPs immediately react to the consequence.

The fears that drive narcissistic behavior would seem to be a sort of a "shell" fear. That is, the narcissist fears that people will see a flaw, and we can only assume that this is a precursor in the mental dynamic of the narcissist to a more fundamental fear. We don't know if this fear is a fear of abandonment as BPs tend to have, or is some other fear or combination of fears, like a non-specific fear of punishment. In both cases, though, the fear is not a cognitive fear. That is, it does not arise from a rational thought process in the disordered person's mind, but rather originates in a lower level of processing that is not under cognitive control.

Narcissists attempt to cope and adjust. Their reactions, while they can be brutal, are generally stabilizing to their view of the situation. Narcissists adapt to their threatening world, creating a space in which they are able to function and fend off the threats they perceive.

Borderlines, in contrast, are much more likely to lapse into despair. BPs may have lifelong patterns of seeking others to care for them. They may find this care in intimate relationships. They may also seek this care through frequent requests for medical care. Where a narcissist appears strong, capable, and independent, BPs often appear vulnerable, weak, in need of help and support, and sometimes just plain pathetic. A narcissist would never want your pity; a BP in contrast, would most often relish it.

A narcissistic dynamic appears to be a higher level of defensive system that allows a person to function more effectively and stably in life. For some, this defensive system may be stable for years, But other people seem to "climb up" to a narcissistic level of functioning, but not be able to stably maintain that defensive system. They fall down into a more borderline dynamic and lose ability to cope and function. They may cycle through these states.

It may be that, simply because they are less inherently capable people, they can't stay inside the "flawless" zone they need for the defense to work. When the narcissistic defense falters, there is no longer a safety shield, and the threats from the world now become an imminent danger. Since their self-images are very weak, their fears take over and they experience a borderline reaction of fear, panic, and dysfunction. On the low functioning extreme, people who are purely borderline are never capable of mustering a narcissistic defense and live with constant fears and dysfunction identified with that disorder.

Notes

High Functioning Borderline

The official definition of BPD gives an impression of a person having difficulty functioning in life. It's easy to imagine, reading the APA diagnostic criteria, someone with BPD being in a hospital setting. But for many people identified by their SOs as having borderline personality disorder, this picture of a significantly handicapped person does not fit their highly capable nature Later, I'll talk about what I call the "my disorder" exaggerations. These exaggerations in published descriptions of personality disorders cause people to throw too broad a net, and label people with personality disorders that may not be correct. This I believe has happened with borderline personality disorder.

When people are labeled with disorders they don't have, something has to stretch to make things agree. This has led to the informal concept of a "high functioning borderline" or "high functioning BP". The idea here is essentially that the diagnostic definition was made too limited and BPs who are "high functioning" are capable of functioning in a way that is still disordered, yet doesn't really reflect the dysfunction inherent in the definition of BPD. At other times they may fall back into a pattern more reflective of low-level functioning suggested by the APA definition.

I believe this entire concept is based on a misunderstanding. A "high functioning BP" is a disordered person, but I believe such a person is actually a narcissist, or at least someone operating in a narcissist mode when "high functioning." A person who's psychological dynamics are limited to a pure borderline dynamic will not have any significant periods of "high functioning." Someone seriously affected with BPD will in fact reflect the diagnostic definition and have difficulty functioning in day-to-day life. If such a person gets better, they move more toward healthy behavior and not toward the higher functioning but still disordered behavior of narcissism.

If you have been exposed to the idea of a "high functioning BP", stop and revisit your experience. Test the high functioning periods that you're thinking of against the definition of narcissism given above. Chances are you'll find that the disordered person you're thinking of is functioning under a narcissistic dynamic during those "high functioning" times.

Notes

A Disorder of Fearlessness - Sociopathy

At one extreme of fear are BPD and NPD, both of which are motivated by intense and disruptive fears. The lives of BPs and narcissists revolve around avoiding and neutralizing situations that stimulate this fear.

At the opposite extreme is the disorder most often known as sociopathy. The clinical name for this disorder is antisocial personality disorder (APD), and it also goes by yet another name: psychopathy. Those who suffer from APD, who I'll call sociopaths, have a huge fear *missing* from their psychological dynamic. Sociopaths have what can perhaps be described as a brain function deficit: they lack all sense of value and concern for other people. Where normal people have a natural fear of causing harm to other people, a sociopath has no such fear or concern. Normal people dread hurting someone else, especially someone emotionally close, and may exert great effort to avoid such hurt or to make it right once it has happened. Moreover, if a normal person does hurt someone else, they will feel remorse afterward.

Sociopathy - The Lack of Conscience

Sociopaths, on the other hand, have no such fears. It simply does not matter to sociopaths what happens to other people, including their family members and intimate partners, nor does it matter who or what causes the harm. Their brains simply lack the connections that would lead to these thoughts and feelings. A sociopath might appear to care about others, or fear hurting others, but the fear is entirely self-centered. A sociopath is not at all bothered by the hurt felt by someone else. Any effort they make to avoid such hurt is simply to make their own lives easier.

Sociopaths also lack an ability to feel a sense of fulfillment as normal people can. Their indifference toward others doesn't just stop negative feelings and fears, but also prevents them from finding joy and satisfaction in relating to others. This leaves them feeling empty, and one thing that fills this void is a thrill. Sociopaths take risks for the sheer satisfaction of having positive feelings. And since they value others very little, they take others along on their risky undertakings.

Narcissists and BPs are driven by a need to find safety; to reduce their level of fear. Sociopaths are different. Sociopaths are simply about self-gratification in a world without interpersonal warmth and satisfaction. And because sociopaths lack remorse or value for others, the things they will choose to do to obtain that gratification are significantly different from what most people would even consider. In the general sense, as long as they can get away with it, sociopaths will do anything that serves their desires.

If hurting another person serves their self gratifying needs, but they perceive that the hassle from that hurtful action will be too great, they will choose not to do it. The balance always rests on the impact on a sociopath. Others have no value to a sociopath.

Notes

Blended Disorders

Personality disorders are hardly an exact science. We talk about them as discrete and identifiable, but in fact a personality disorder is defined as a combination of thoughts, emotions, and behaviors. These can have infinite variations, and in reality no one will ever perfectly match any disorder definition.

The people who made these disorder definitions recognized this. In addition to the 10 personality disorders which have specific diagnostic definitions, there is also a diagnosis for "personality disorder not otherwise specified." This can be used in a case where a person's overall functioning is disordered, there are traits of several different personality disorders present, yet the person does not meet the criteria for any specific personality disorder. A common example might be someone who shows characteristics of both BPD and NPD, but not enough to diagnose with either disorder alone. (These diagnostic definitions are included later.)

As I've described above, I commonly hear descriptions of partners who have both BPD and NPD behaviors, often cycling from one to the other. It's not so important to have a precise label in cases like this. What is important is to recognize that such a person is disordered, and to learn and apply whatever knowledge is available about the disorders that appear to be relevant to the person's behavior.

Notes

Defense Mechanisms - Patterns in Responding

When we live with someone with an abusive personality disorder, especially if we're their spouse, we often wonder if *we* are the crazy one. This is because ordinary reality can be terribly frightening to disordered abusers, and they develop a number of defense mechanisms which alter their reality to make it less frightening to them. Defense mechanisms are subconsciously controlled deviations from the normal way that events are perceived and remembered. The result is a reality perceived by the disordered person which has been altered to make it less threatening.

As you may remember, both narcissists and BPs have intense and irrational fears which are based in their perception and interpretation of events. Events and situations which present no particular difficulty for you or me can be perceived as terribly threatening to those with these disorders. Since the fears are a response not to real threats, but rather interpreted threats, the danger can be eliminated by simply not perceiving the threat. If a truck were about to run you over – a real threat – and you try to eliminate this threat by not perceiving it, your efforts would be short-lived. But because the threat to these disordered people is only perceived, it can be stopped by blocking perception. One dysfunction – the irrational fear triggered by a perceived event– is countered by another dysfunction – a defense mechanism that alters that perception.

These defense mechanisms are not rational, cognitive processes with a basis in logical thought. They are mental processes, but they operate at a level below awareness: a subconscious level. These defense mechanisms actually can alter the functioning of the mind to protect the person from threatening situations.

If we are an important part of the disordered person's life, conflict arises between their reality and our reality. To maintain their reality, they continually try to distort our reality to match theirs. Their distortions may be very obvious to a healthy person – if they can be observed. However we are not always aware of these distortions until they become the subject of discussion or action.

Consistent with both the narcissist's and BP's intense fears, defense mechanisms can be understood as ways that the disordered person's reality can be altered so that it is not so frightening. For someone with narcissistic defenses, these defenses tend to make flaws either disappear or shift to others. For those with the borderline dynamic, these defenses can sometimes eliminate the suggestion that a significant person will abandon the BP, or they may alter the importance of the abandoning person to make it less threatening for that person to abandon the BP.

Dissociation - Altered Perception

Disordered abusers often recall things completely differently from healthy people, or in some cases fail to recall things at all. They do this with complete conviction, a conviction which causes the healthy people around them to question their own recall and clarity of mind.

In most cases, the abuser is not lying. They are absolutely convinced of their recall and they truly remember events as they say. They are not consciously distorting what they know and they are not lying. Their understanding of what transpired in the past is truly different from yours or mine. This can be extremely confusing to someone living with the disordered person.

These differences in their recall arise from two elements of a defense mechanism called dissociation. One is an inability to properly perceive certain threatening events or situations. The second is an inability to recall events which are now threatening.

Selective Observation

The first part of the defense of dissociation is a distortion in perception. Standing in the same place, looking at the same actions, listening to the same words, you or I may perceive something entirely differently from a disordered person.

How could this be?

Remember that very small events, with no significance to you or me, can signal a terrifying threat to a disordered person. Just to give an example of how bizarre these connections can be, you might say to someone with BPD, "Wow, you've been busy lately." The BPs mind may process this – in a way that isn't consciously understood – along these lines: "He said I'm busy. He said that because he saw that my apartment is messy. He thinks I'm a total slob. He's never going to talk to me again." To a BP, this is terrifying.

So the tiniest of events can be a source of terror. To protect themselves from the horrible feelings these fears cause, dissociation can simply block the perception of the event. "You said what? No you didn't." Their minds do not allow some sensory signals to enter their awareness. Or their perception may be distorted to make the event less threatening.

When recalling a situation whose perception has been altered in this way, the disordered person is not aware of the true events that took place. They only remember what has been allowed to pass through their perception. They believe that what they perceived is the complete and correct event. It should be no surprise then, that they will emphatically argue that their perception is correct.

Notes

Diminished Recall

A second aspect of dissociation helps to reduce painful memories. A threatening situation maybe observed by a disordered person and yet still be properly perceived and recorded in their memory. Later, because of new information or because of a change in the emotional state of the disordered person, that memory may become very threatening to them.

To ward off the pain caused by this fear, the defense mechanism of dissociation may prevent the recall of that event. This operates below the level of awareness, in the subconscious mind. This is commonly seen in trauma survivors. It protects them from the terrifying memories of their trauma. For the disordered with unreasonable fears, dissociation can protect them from the memory of threatening situations or events.

Notes

Automatic Processing Is Not Dissociation

Dissociation should not be confused with automatic processing. In descriptions of dissociation, you may hear the example of driving on a familiar route and later having no recall of driving. The same could be said about walking up a flight of stairs or controlling hundreds of other movements or actions that we make in the course of our lives. This is *not* dissociation. This is called automatic processing, and represents a level of control we can all normally develop, which functions without cognitive (thought-based) control. In automatic processing, the stimulus needed to perform the action is not thought about and thus is not remembered. For example, we have no recall of what sensations we respond to in maintaining our balance as we walk. Yet we know that we must perceive sensory input and process it or we would fall over.

Automatic processing is a normal and healthy process, and enables us to do things easily which might otherwise require our complete and exhaustive concentration. It is completely different from dissociation, which is an inability to recall something which actually has been observed and remembered.

Denial

Denial is simply the assertion by a disordered person that something is not so, when ordinary observation or common sense confirms that it is so. Technically, denial is probably a manifestation of the defense mechanism of dissociation. Dissociation blocks the perception or recall of events. When this altered awareness is expressed as reality, we see denial. Anything that is threatening to a disordered person may be denied in this way, thus protecting the person from the feelings caused by that threat.

Notes

Rationalization

As we've seen, narcissists act aggressively to avoid any suggestion of a flaw. Rationalization is an assertion, nominally based in logic, that argues that the flaw doesn't exist - or if it does exist, that it isn't the narcissist's flaw. Rationalization can also argue that the flaw is the responsibility of anyone *other* than the narcissist.

Rationalization may be convoluted or obscure, because it often flies in the face of observable facts. When the rationalization is confusing, it distracts from the observable reality and focuses attention on the logic of the rationalization. This can make it easier for the disordered person to prevail in their argument, since it is simply too difficult or impossible to refute.

Notes

Projection

Projection is another unconsciously motivated defense mechanism that is often seen in those with abusive disorders. In projection, a disordered person perceives their problem to be present in another person rather than themselves. The typical occurrence can be described simply, "There are two people and a problem present. I'm safe when I have no problems, therefore you are the one with this problem." Projection is likely to be seen or not seen depending on a particular situation. Because it involves an assertion by the disordered person, it is something we only see in conversation.

Projection is also a dysfunction in perception. However, unlike the defenses of memory described above, in projection the quality or event being projected is recognized by the disordered person. Distortion occurs in the *placement* of that quality or event. Consistent with the narcissistic defense of maintaining an image without flaws, a quality or event which is perceived to be flawed and actually resides with disordered person is displaced by projection to reside with someone else.

My observation is that disordered people prefer to rationalize a flawed behavior or quality rather than to project it. Where possible, a disordered person will expend considerable energy to create a rational defense for the perceived flaw. Projection seems to come into play when a flaw is serious and undeniable, and it is difficult or impossible to rationalize the flaw.

Notes

Splitting

Splitting means to view people or things with extreme positive or negative value. For example, a disordered spouse may at times express that you are wonderful, and at other times express that you are terrible.

Splitting is a defense typically seen in someone with a borderline dynamic. Splitting someone in a positive way enhances that person's emotional value as a secure partner. That is, when a BP perceives an intimate partner as someone they can depend on not to leave them, splitting them positive exaggerates the good qualities of that person. Then, having such a wonderful person as a reliable partner increases the feeling of safety for the BP.

Splitting someone in a negative way can have the effect of defusing or disarming the pain of being abandoned by that person. Thus, if the BP perceives that an intimate partner is about to abandon them, attributing horrible qualities to that person makes the abandonment become a positive outcome. After all, no one wants a horrible person as an intimate partner and a source of emotional security.

Bear in mind, BP's perceive threats of abandonment based on minute and often irrelevant signals. We may have no idea that a BP has picked up such a suggestion, because the cues they respond to may have no meaning to us, and we simply don't notice them. The BP, however, observes and responds in proportion to their tremendous level of fear. Thus, a BP may abruptly and inexplicably split us negative. The result can be extremely puzzling and upsetting to the person being split.

Splitting can also take an extreme form which I informally call "splitting out of existence." Splitting often can be situational, and with a little time and reassurance a BP's perspective may return to something more usual for them. In some situations, though, the negative splitting may be extreme, complete, and permanent.

In this case, the BP may permanently refuse to recognize the existence of the other person. He/she may refuse all interaction, and simply act as if the other person isn't there. This again represents a distortion of reality to make things safer for the BP. After all, you can't be abandoned by someone who doesn't exist. It is, however, extremely painful for a partner in an intimate relationship to be "split out of existence" by the person they love.

Splitting someone in a negative way can also be a reflection of a narcissistic defense. It may happen in response to another person revealing a flaw about the disordered person. Consistent with the narcissistic defense described above, a narcissist may demean and devalue the person revealing a flaw. This is equivalent to splitting someone in a negative way.

Notes

Blame Shifting

Blame shifting is another defense mechanism based on distortion of reality. It is also fundamentally narcissistic. Blame shifting is simply the rational or irrational assertion that the responsibility for problems lies in someone other than the disordered person. Blame shifting is often used by disordered people when a partner confronts them about their abusive or neglectful behavior.

Rather than distorting the reality of what has happened, this defense mechanism focuses attention away from the person responsible for what has happened, and distorts reality to direct that responsibility toward someone other than the disordered person. This can be viewed as a combination of the defenses rationalization and projection.

Notes

Mirroring

Mirroring is more of a behavior than a defense mechanism, but it is similar in that it also functions at a level below rational thought and choice. In mirroring, a person adapts their behavior and presentation to "mirror back" to us the qualities which they perceive that we desire to see. Most disordered abusers are extremely good at mirroring, and have an extraordinary ability to perceive what we desire.

Mirroring is an adaptive technique which helps narcissists to maintain an image of flawlessness. By showing us all the qualities they believe we wish to see in them, narcissists can make themselves extremely acceptable to us. More than just avoiding having any flaws, mirroring can make us believe that the narcissists is a truly wonderful person. This is an extremely safe situation for narcissists.

Mirroring itself may not cause great harm to us. It can, however, lead us to make wrong judgments about narcissists, something which serves their purpose but generally not our own. Mirroring in the early stages of a romantic relationship can prove devastating, by drawing us into strong romantic attraction to a façade of personality. This is discussed in greater detail in the section called "The Ins and Outs of Narcissism".

Notes

Brainwashing

A disordered person's reality is very different from a normal person's. The disordered person's safety rests on maintaining the believability of that reality. When an intimate partner or spouse becomes an important part of the disordered person's life, a conflict in realities occurs. To eliminate this threat to their safety, disordered abusers often use the same techniques used in brainwashing.

Brainwashing is a process of tearing down a person's reality and replacing it with a different one. Some of the components are: isolating the victim; denying the victim's reality; depriving the victim of sleep; sending consistent messages with great emotional force; making the victim feel unsafe; and wearing the victim down. Repetition is essential to brainwashing.

Notes

Raging and Intimidation

There is nothing subtle about the brute force intimidation used by disordered abusers. On its face, this kind of behavior is not based on disordered thoughts or reactions directly. However, only the tremendous distress of the fears of the disordered could motivate such cruel and crushing behavior.

Because raging may seem to be a state where the person is out of control, it might not look at first blush like a defense mechanism. However, many rages are not just an expression of the intensity of fear, they are also intended to control the person who is the target of the rage. As we saw with brainwashing, the disordered have a powerful need to maintain the believability of their distorted reality.

Rages are terrifying to a normal person, and most of us would agree that we would go to great lengths to stop a rage directed at us. In effect, the abuser transfers their intense fear to us by raging, and this enmeshes us in their disordered level of reaction to the world. Rages punish us for doing or saying things that threaten the abuser.

Moreover, even though we are not consciously aware of it, rages condition us to respond fearfully to the abuser. Over time, we become much less likely to repeat the assertions or the behaviors that have triggered rages in the past. Thus, raging and intimidation can help to stabilize the distorted reality of the abuser, and while not necessarily changing the very short-term situation as some of the other defense mechanisms do, they definitely do act to support the abusers reality.

Substance Abuse & Disorders

Because disordered abusers suffer from both self-loathing and terrifying fear, they live with constant psychological stress and pain. Substances that can reduce this pain can be very attractive to them. Many disordered abusers self-medicate. The most commonly used drug is alcohol. Marijuana, prescription drugs, and other illegal drugs are also used by abusers, and combinations are common.

Unfortunately, by their nature, such substances are both addictive and ineffective in the long-term. Over time, tolerance develops, and larger and larger quantities of the substance are needed to achieve the same impact. Over time, disordered abusers can easily progress to using large amounts of substances on a regular basis.

The regular abuse of substances in large amounts has two effects which anyone living with a substance abuser needs to understand.

Reduced Inhibition

The first effect that is important to understand is a result of using high doses of substances at one time. Large doses of substances cause a significant reduction in inhibition. While we might have an image of a smiling drunk, such a pleasant outcome is not going to be the case when you reduce the inhibitions of someone that has BPD, NPD or sociopathy.

Bear in mind, such people are dealing with very strong emotions and are constantly striving to maintain a safe situation. They are constantly using self-control to make their world safe.

Clearly, when they abuse substances at a level that significantly reduces anxiety and inhibition, it is also going to reduce their level of self-control. This translates into a deterioration of behavior which has two consequences. First, it is extremely unpleasant for those of us living with the abuser because they tend to be more abusive and less controlled. Second, it reduces the effectiveness of the abuser's coping strategies, which depend to some degree on the abuser's self-control. That means the world is going to become less safe for the abuser because of their impaired self-control. Threats will appear more dangerous, and violent reactions to small suggestions can be expected.

Although the substance is being used to reduce anxiety and fear, ironically it results in an increase in both. This makes things worse not just for the abuser but also for those close to them.

Notes

Deterioration of Mental Function

The second effect of prolonged, large quantity substance abuse is a substantial deterioration in overall mental function. This impairment has been compared to schizophrenia, in that it results in a deterioration of personality and mental acuity.

Since those with personality disorders are already struggling with deficits in their personality, the further impairment from long-term substance abuse makes a bad situation even worse.

This deterioration is long-term, and does not come and go with daily fluctuations in the level of substances in the abusers body. Its effects may be permanent, or they may persist long after a substance abuser becomes clean and sober, with very little change initially and then a gradual improvement over the course of perhaps a year or two years.

This is important to understand, because sobriety is not an immediate solution, merely a step toward improvement in the future.

Meaning from Madness

Notes

Treatment Outlook

A big part of understanding how to deal with these disorders in a partner comes from having some idea what the future may hold. Personality disorders are manifested in stable characteristics of the person. But those characteristics are not unchangeable.

As recently as a few years ago, personality disorders were considered to be difficult to treat or even hopeless. BPD, in particular, has a popular reputation as being intractable. But according to Sperry in his 2003 book on diagnosis and treatment of personality disorders, current thinking is much more optimistic. Clinical perspectives today hold that all personality disorders can be improved with treatment. The biggest single determining factor for success in the treatment of personality disorders is the patient's acceptance and motivation to change. Thus, today a personality disordered patient who is motivated to improve through therapy has a good chance of improvement, and potential for much improvement.

Given that, the treatment outlook is different for each of these three disorders.

Borderline

According to Sperry and the DSM-IV TR, the

most optimistic outlook among the three abusive personality disorders is actually for the disorder with a reputation for being intractable: BPD. This reflects a major change in thought among clinicians over the past ten years. Most BPs openly admit that they are in pain. While their disordered thoughts and emotions are deeply ingrained, as is true for all personality disorders, BPs are amenable to treatment because they can recognize and, at least to some extent, deal with their problems. This is reflected in the predominant characteristic of BPD: a fear of abandonment, which shows that BPs recognize they have characteristics that are intolerable in most intimate relationships.

However, as I described above, I think that many people who are thought to have BPD (including "high functioning BPs) are really functioning with the fundamental dynamic of narcissism. As you'll see below, the realistic outlook for narcissism is not the same as for BPD.

Narcissism

Narcissists are in pain, which is clear from their extreme behavior within safe intimate relationships. They know this, and at some level many narcissists must privately recognize that they are ill and suffering. Yet the treatment outlook for narcissism is not good.

An active and functioning narcissist maintains

an outer perimeter defense which is free from any observable flaws. Of course, it makes no sense whatever to fix something when there is nothing that one can see that is wrong. To simply enter treatment is an admission by the narcissist that something is wrong with them, which is terribly destabilizing and threatening.

This alone is enough to prevent them from seeking or accepting treatment. Narcissists who enter individual treatment generally can be expected to exit the treatment fairly quickly, rationalizing their decision and shifting blame to the mental health professional.

Sometimes family members, especially spouses, of narcissists may succeed in physically getting their narcissistic family member into a therapeutic setting. But the sole premise for the narcissist's appearance there is to facilitate the fixing of problems in anyone except the narcissist.

Couple counseling, when one of the couple is a narcissist, is often disastrous for the other partner. The knowledge and credibility of the mental health professional in assessing dysfunctional behavior presents a tremendous threat to the narcissist's safety shield of a perfect image. Narcissists in this situation typically muster all of their abilities to distort and influence in order to convince the counselor that the problems reside entirely with the other partner. In the short interactions of a few counseling sessions, mental health professionals are often unable to see through these narcissistic distortions. The distortions are often accepted by the counselor, and partners of narcissists often suffer further emotional harm from improper counseling.

Sociopathy

The most perplexing issue is the treatment of a sociopath. The crux of the issue here is that, regardless of what *we* may think, the sociopath is not suffering from their disorder. To the sociopath there is nothing wrong and moreover, there is no illness to deny. Everything is fine and everything feels fine. People around the sociopath may be troubled, even deeply troubled, by the sociopath's behavior. To the sociopath, this is everybody else's problem. It presents no difficulty to the sociopath and there is neither reason nor motivation to change. And, as Sperry reports, sociopaths rarely enter treatment by choice.

Moreover, sociopathy as we understand it has a different underlying causal mechanism than either BPD or narcissism. Both BPD and narcissism appear to involve learned adaptations in interpreting and responding to the actions of other people. These patterns of perceiving and responding are deeply ingrained but they are amenable to change if the disordered person is motivated.

Sociopathy, on the other hand, appears to involve something more like a physical loss of function of a certain portion of the brain. In other words, sociopaths appear to be innately incapable of feeling remorse or responsibility. It is not that they have adaptively learned not to respond with remorse, but rather their minds are simply not wired to produce such a response. If this is the case, teaching and retraining may well be useless when dealing with a person whose problem is purely sociopathy.

Notes

Sperry, Len, M.D, Ph.D, *Handbook of Diagnosis and Treatment of DSM-IV-TR Personality Disorders, second edition*; Brunner-Routledge, New York, 2003.

APA Diagnostic Definitions

For the US, the American Psychiatric
Association (APA) oversees the process of
defining what mental illnesses are, how you
identify them, and what they're called. The
APA publishes a weighty and expensive
document entitled *Diagnostic and Statistical
Manual of Mental Disorders, 4th Edition-Text
Revision.* For our purposes, the important
content of the DSM is what they call the
diagnostic criteria for the disorders.

These criteria specify the characteristics that
need to be observed to diagnose a person as
having a mental disorder, and they are written
for clinicians who are diagnosing and treating
patients. Nevertheless, they are reasonably free
of psychological jargon and they generally make
sense to most people. This is not to say that
they are simple, because differentiating one
disorder from another is not a simple task.
However, substantial meaning and
understanding can be gained from these criteria
without an education in psychology or
psychiatry.

I believe that the "essential dynamics" that I
have described earlier in this work can be very
helpful in differentiating the disorders. They can
serve as a frame of reference for understanding
what a disordered person is doing, and they can
also serve as a pointer to a particular disorder

with which that person may be diagnosed.

Still, the true and ultimate test of whether a person has any particular mental disorder rests in the application of these diagnostic criteria from the DSM. For that reason, I think it is important that anyone with a serious concern about these illnesses should read and evaluate these criteria.

I often hear people admonish themselves that they are not trained professionals and they should not try to diagnose someone as having a personality disorder. When the person in question is a spouse or fills another important role in your life, I disagree. I certainly hope no one will try to *treat* a spouse or family member. But it's *essential* to have some idea what is going on when a loved one or significant other has serious problems.

When you can establish, if only in your own mind, that the SO's behavior matches a specific disorder, you can then deal with the situation in a factual way. You can understand what behaviors are typical, what treatment options are available, and what outcomes can be expected. This understanding is essential to making good decisions about how to deal with a situation that is always painful and confusing.

There is a second and very important reason that family members and SOs should try to make an informal diagnosis. Diagnosis requires information – information about the disordered person's long term behavior patterns. But it is impossible for a clinician to get good information in a few sessions with someone, especially when that person denies that they are ill. This is why people who fit BPD, NPD, or sociopathy are often misdiagnosed during their mental health treatment (which is often brief). The same distortions used with spouses and family members are used with clinicians.

It is actually the spouse and family who have the proper depth of understanding to test the diagnostic criteria. So use your experience and judgment, and you should be able to develop useful and reliable conclusions from the diagnostic criteria.

Notes

General Criteria for Personality Disorder

Each of the personality disorders has its own unique thought and behavior patterns. But in order to be considered a personality disorder, as opposed to some other type of illness like a mood disorder (of which depression is a commonly known example), certain general characteristics must be met.

In simple terms, a person with a personality disorder has thoughts, feelings, and impulsive reactions which are significantly different from what is normal in their culture. This pattern of inner experience and behavior doesn't change much across differing situations, and it causes significant distress or impairment in life functioning.

General Diagnostic Criteria for a Personality Disorder

DSM-IV-TR General Criteria for a Personality Disorder

A. An enduring pattern of inner experience and behavior that deviates markedly from the expectations of the individual's culture. This pattern is manifested in one (or more) of the following areas:

(1) cognition (i.e., ways of perceiving and interpreting self, other people, and events)

(2) affectivity (i.e., the range, intensity, liability, and appropriateness of the emotional response)

(3) interpersonal functioning

(4) impulse control

B. The enduring pattern is inflexible and pervasive across a broad range of personal and social situations.

C. The enduring pattern leads to clinically significant distress or impairment in social, occupational, or other important areas of functioning.

D. The pattern is stable and of long duration, and its onset can be traced back at least to adolescence or early adulthood.

E. The enduring pattern is not better accounted for as a manifestation or consequence of another mental disorder.

F. The enduring pattern is not due to the direct physiological effects of a substance (e.g., a drug of abuse, a medication) or general medical condition (e.g., head trauma).

From *Diagnostic and Statistical Manual of Mental Disorders, 4th Edition-Text Revision.* Copyright 2000. American Psychiatric Association.

Borderline Personality Disorder

DSM-IV-TR Criteria for Borderline Personality Disorder (301.83)

A pervasive pattern of instability of interpersonal relationships, self-image, affect, and control over impulses beginning by early adulthood and present in a variety of contexts, as indicated by at least five of the following:

(1)   frantic efforts to avoid real or imagined abandonment. Note: do not include suicidal or self-mutilation behavior covered in criteria 5

(2)   a pattern of unstable and intense interpersonal relationships characterized by alternating between extremes of idealization and devaluation

(3)   identity disturbance: persistent and markedly disturbed, distorted or unstable self-image or sense of self

(4)   impulsivity in at least two areas that are potentially self-damaging (e.g., spending, sex, substance abuse, reckless driving, binge eating). Note: do not include suicidal or self-mutilating behavior covered in criterion 5

(5)   recurrent suicidal behavior, gestures, or threats, or self-mutilating behavior

(6)   affective instability due to a marked reactivity of mood (e.g., intense episodic dysphoria, irritability, or anxiety usually lasting

a few hours and only rarely more than a few days)

(7)   chronic feelings of emptiness

(8)   inappropriate, intense anger or lack of control of anger (e.g., frequent displays of temper, constant anger, recurrent physical fights)

(9)   transient, stress-related paranoid ideation or severe dissociative symptoms.

From *Diagnostic and Statistical Manual of Mental Disorders, 4th Edition-Text Revision.* Copyright 2000. American Psychiatric Association.

Notes

Narcissistic Personality Disorder

DSM-IV-TR Criteria for Narcissistic Personality Disorder (301.81)

A pervasive pattern of grandiosity (in fantasy or behavior), need for admiration, and lack of empathy, beginning by early adulthood and present in a variety of contexts, as indicated by five (or more) of the following:

(1) has a grandiose sense of self-importance (e.g., exaggerates achievements and talents, expects to be recognized as superior without commensurate achievements)

(2) preoccupation with fantasies of unlimited success, power, brilliance, beauty, or ideal love

(3) believes that he or she is "special" and unique and can only be understood by, or should associate with, other special or high-status people (or institutions)

(4) requires excessive admiration

(5) a sense of entitlement, i.e., unreasonable expectations of especially favorable treatment or automatic compliance with his or her expectations

(6) is interpersonally exploitative, i.e., takes advantage of others to achieve his or her own ends

(7) lack of empathy: unwilling to recognize or identify with the feelings and needs of others

(8) is often envious of others or believes that others are envious of him or her

(9) arrogant, haughty behaviors or attitudes.

From *Diagnostic and Statistical Manual of*

Mental Disorders, 4th Edition-Text Revision.
Copyright 2000. American Psychiatric
Association.

Notes

Sociopathy: Antisocial Personality Disorder

DSM-IV-TR Criteria For Antisocial Personality
Disorder (301.70)

A. There is a pervasive pattern of disregard for
and violation of the rights of others occurring
since age 15, as indicated by at least three of the
following:

(1)   failure to conform to social
norms with respect to lawful behaviors as
indicated by repeatedly performing acts that
are grounds for arrest

(2)   irritability and aggressiveness, as
indicated by repeated physical fights or

assaults

(3)　　　　consistent irresponsibility, as indicated by repeated failure to sustain consistent work behavior or honor financial obligations

(4)　　　　impulsivity or failure to plan ahead

(5)　　　　deceitfulness, as indicated by repeated lying, use of aliases, or conning others for personal profit or pleasure.

(6)　　　　reckless disregard for safety of self or others

(7)　　　　lack of remorse, as indicated by being indifferent to or rationalizing having hurt, mistreated, or stolen from another.

B.　the individual is at least 18 years old.

C.　There is evidence of conduct disorder with onset before age 15.

D.　Occurrence of antisocial behavior is not exclusively during the course of schizophrenia or a manic episode.

From *Diagnostic and Statistical Manual of Mental Disorders, 4th Edition-Text Revision.* Copyright 2000. American Psychiatric Association.

For　Notes

Meaning from Madness

The "My Disorder" Exaggerations

In the popular literature about personality disorders (in which this book must be included) there is a trend which I've tried to avoid. In an effort to describe the experience of knowing someone with a personality disorder, some authors will tend to include characteristics they believe are frequently present in such people. In doing so, they're able to make a larger and more complete description of a person then by limiting themselves to the DSM diagnostic criteria that strictly define these disorders.

Unfortunately, these are often personal qualities that don't differentiate between different personality disorders. In fact, they don't differentiate between people who have a disorder and those who don't. For example you may read that people with sociopathy are extremely charming people. However, you may read the same thing about people with BPD – and NPD. And of course you certainly will find the same quality in many people who aren't disordered at all.

The result is that these definitions tend to cast far too broad a net. For people who are just learning about personality disorders for the first time, it may lead them to believe a particular disorder applies to their partner or family member. Unfortunately, the qualities that are being used to make this decision aren't unique to that disorder. This can mean people newly learning about personality disorders may incorrectly identify the particular disorder that is affecting their partner.

A better way of bringing these characteristics into the picture might be to say this: though personality disorders are very serious illnesses and cause major problems to the people who suffer with them, you might be surprised to learn that those people may also have strikingly positive qualities. We may have a stereotypical idea of the mentally ill as being nonfunctional in all aspects of life. But in reality, the personality disordered may show strikingly positive qualities that seem in conflict with the seriousness of their illness.

This is the main reason that I've chosen to include the DSM diagnostic criteria in this short book. The diagnostic criteria are the authoritative definition of these disorders. And as you may have seen, they do not include qualities like being charming, attractive, or successful.

There *are* some nonspecific characteristics that can help us understand personality disorders. For example, I talked earlier about how narcissism often leads people to be extremely successful in whenever they do in their lives. It is helpful to know these things because they help to make sense of the entire picture. But they are not definitive and don't differentiate between people who have a disorder and don't have a disorder.

The essential dynamic that I've described for each of these disorders does reflect the specific and unique pattern of perception and thought for these disorders. And while not the complete or official definition, they should not lead you to identify these disorders where they do not exist. It is useful to review the DSM criteria to see if they confirm whatever conclusion you make from applying the essential dynamics.

For   Notes

Conclusion

The behavior of people with the abusive personality disorders – narcissistic, borderline, and sociopathic – is puzzling and brutal. Their incessant attempts to alter our perceptions of reality make it even more difficult to assess and deal with.

People with both borderline and narcissistic personality disorder are driven by intense and irrational fears, while sociopaths try to fill an emotional void without the constraint of conscience or empathy. To cope with the emotional pain they endure, all three groups develop subconscious psychological defense mechanism, which allow them to redefine their world and their reality to be less painful for them. Substance abuse adds fuel to this emotional fire; a fuel which continues to burn even after the abuse stops. Yet because of their intelligence, outward composure, and assertive arguments, it can be difficult to understand what is really happening with them and us.

When we recognize the underlying motivations of these disorders, and learn the patterns that emerge from the common defense mechanisms they use, we have the tools we need to distance ourselves from their distortions and build our own understanding of the situation – one based on reality and not on distortion.

The possibilities for improvement in these disorders with effective treatment are much better than commonly believed. New multi-dimensional treatments combine medication, skills training, and different therapeutic interactions. These treatments depend for success on the commitment of the patient to make changes and improve. Committed patients with BPD have good chance of major improvement. Committed narcissists also have moderate prospects for significant change. Even sociopaths can improve with treatment, though few will enter treatment or effectively engage once there.

Taken together, understanding what drives disordered behavior and knowing the prospects for change give us a way to paint a picture of our future with a disordered person. That picture needs to be combined with a searching look into our own emotions and needs. When we put these pieces together, we often find a confident understanding of the decisions we need to make and the path we need to follow. My book *Tears and Healing, The journey to the light after an abusive relationship*, guides you through the process of searching and defining your needs and your life visions.

For many, the third piece in this puzzle is the attraction that drew us into a relationship with a disordered person in the first place. Too often, we view ourselves as helpless leaves bobbing along on a chaotic torrent of emotion that we call being in love. But there is a purpose and pattern in the way our minds work to put us in love with someone. By understanding these, we can make conscious choices to set ourselves up in situations so that we end up in love with the right people, in happier relationships, and relationships that endure. My book *In Love and Loving It – Or Not!, A User's Guide to Love and Falling in Love* explains how and why our minds work to get us in love, what we can do to make that work better for us, and how we can make sure we get the love we need to stay happy and healthy.

Reflecting the paradigm shift the internet has brought in many aspects of commerce, these books are not generally available in stores, but can be purchased online at

http://dalkeithpress.com/

Tears and Healing, Meaning from Madness, and *In Love and Loving It – Or Not!* offer you my collective experience on the major challenges of dealing with a relationship that became abusive, defining where your life needs to go, and moving yourself toward that goal.

You may also enjoy my philosophical work, *The Way of Respect – Ancient Wisdom Adapted for Today*. An interpretation and restatement of the ancient Chinese Tao te Ching, or way of life, this enduring work uses paradox and contradiction to teach us principles and approaches for success in interactions with others, especially as leaders of others.

Index